200 + Powerful Affirmations for a Healthier You by 100RAB

Introduction:

Welcome to this book on healthy affirmations! If you're here, it means you're interested in living a healthier and more fulfilling life. You know that your thoughts and beliefs shape your reality, and that by changing your mindset, you can achieve the results you desire.

This book contains 200 powerful affirmations that will help you cultivate a positive and healthy mindset. Each affirmation is accompanied by an explanation of its meaning and a practical tip on how to use it in your daily life.

By reading and repeating these affirmations regularly, you'll train your mind to focus on what you want and attract more of it into your life. You'll also become more aware of your habits and behaviors and make healthier choices that support your well-being.

So, are you ready to embark on a journey of self-discovery and transformation? Let's begin!

THE ULTIMATE TRUTH

I AM NOT THE BODY

I AM NOT THE MIND

Chapter 1: Affirmations for Physical Health

ॐ (Om)

- ✓ I am healthy and strong.

- ✓ I nourish my body with wholesome food and plenty of water.

- ✓ I move my body daily and enjoy the benefits of exercise.

- ✓ I breathe deeply and fill my lungs with fresh air.

- ✓ I am grateful for my body and treat it with kindness and compassion.

- ✓ I listen to my body's needs and honor them.

- ✓ I am flexible and adaptable, and can handle any challenge that comes my way.

- ✓ I rest when I need to and allow my body to recharge.

- ✓ I trust my body's ability to heal and regenerate.

Chapter 2: Affirmations for Mental Health

ॐ (Om)

- ✓ I am worthy of love and respect.

- ✓ I am in control of my thoughts and emotions.

- ✓ I let go of negativity and embrace positivity.

- ✓ I am calm and centered, no matter what happens around me.

- ✓ I trust my intuition and make wise decisions.

- ✓ I am intelligent and capable of learning and growing.

- ✓ I am a problem solver and can find solutions to any challenge.

- ✓ I am confident and believe in myself and my abilities.

✓ I am creative and express myself in unique and meaningful ways.

✓ I am optimistic and focus on the good in every situation.

Chapter 3: Affirmations for Emotional Health

ॐ (Om)

- ✓ I express my emotions in a healthy and constructive way.

- ✓ I forgive myself and others for past mistakes and move on with grace.

- ✓ I choose to focus on the good in my life and appreciate it fully.

- ✓ I am surrounded by loving and supportive people who uplift me.

- ✓ I radiate joy and happiness, and attract the same back to me.

- ✓ I am at peace with myself and others.

- ✓ I am patient and kind with myself and others.

- ✓ I am open-minded and willing to see things from different perspectives.

- ✓ I am honest and authentic in all my relationships.

- ✓ I am grateful for the love and connection I share with others.

Chapter 4: Affirmations for Spiritual Health

ॐ (Om)

- ✓ I am connected to the universal energy that flows through all things.

- ✓ I am grateful for the blessings in my life and welcome more abundance.

- ✓ I trust that everything happens for my highest good, even if I don't understand it at the time.

- I take time each day to connect with my inner wisdom and guidance.

- I live my life with purpose and meaning, knowing that I am here to make a positive impact.

- I am in harmony with the universe and its natural rhythms.

- I am open to divine guidance and trust the path that is meant for me.

- I am grateful for the abundance of nature and its healing properties.

- I honor and respect all living beings and the planet we call home.

- I trust that everything is interconnected and that my actions have an impact on the world around me.

- I am open to new experiences and opportunities that align with my values and purpose.

✓ I release any fears or doubts that hold me back from living my best life.

✓ I am at peace with myself and the world, knowing that all is well in this moment.

✓ I find joy and fulfillment in simple moments and experiences.

✓ I am grateful for the journey of life and all the lessons it brings.

✓ I trust the timing and unfolding of my life, knowing that everything happens at the perfect time.

✓ I am open to receiving blessings and opportunities that come my way.

✓ I am guided by my intuition and trust the messages it brings.

✓ I am a co-creator of my life and attract positive experiences and outcomes.

✓ I am grateful for the beauty and wonder of the world and appreciate it fully.

Chapter 5: Affirmations for Relationships

ॐ (Om)

- ✓ I am worthy of love and respect in all my relationships.

- ✓ I am surrounded by loving and supportive people who uplift me.

- ✓ I communicate my needs and feelings clearly and respectfully.

- ✓ I listen attentively to others and show empathy and understanding.

- ✓ I create healthy boundaries that honor my needs and values.

- ✓ I am committed to building positive and fulfilling relationships with others.

- ✓ I forgive myself and others for past mistakes and move on with grace.

- ✓ I am open to new friendships and relationships that align with my values and purpose.

- ✓ I nurture and cherish the relationships that matter to me.

- ✓ I celebrate the differences and uniqueness of others, and learn from them.

Chapter 6: Affirmations for Success and Abundance

ॐ (Om)

- ✓ I am worthy of success and abundance in all areas of my life.

- ✓ I attract opportunities and resources that support my goals and dreams.

✓ I am confident in my abilities and trust my intuition to guide me.

✓ I take action towards my goals with focus and determination.

✓ I believe in myself and my potential to achieve great things.

✓ I am resilient and bounce back from setbacks with grace and strength.

✓ I am open to receiving abundance and blessings from the universe.

✓ I use my resources wisely and make smart financial decisions.

✓ I am grateful for the abundance that surrounds me and appreciate it fully.

✓ I inspire and uplift others with my success and abundance.

<u>**Chapter 7: Affirmations for Self-Care and Self-Love**</u>

ॐ (Om)

- ✓ I prioritize self-care and make time for activities that nourish my body and soul.

- ✓ I treat myself with love and kindness, just as I would a dear friend.

- ✓ I celebrate my accomplishments and give myself credit for the progress I make.

- ✓ I speak to myself with positivity and encouragement.

- ✓ I am comfortable in my own skin and embrace my unique qualities.

✓ I let go of self-criticism and embrace self-acceptance and self-love.

✓ I am worthy of happiness and joy, and allow myself to experience them fully.

✓ I trust myself to make the best decisions for my well-being.

✓ I release any limiting beliefs that hold me back from living my best life.

✓ I am grateful for the journey of self-discovery and self-improvement.

Chapter 8: Affirmations for Gratitude and Positivity

ॐ (Om)

- ✓ I am grateful for the blessings in my life and appreciate them fully.

- ✓ I focus on the good in every situation and find the silver lining.

- ✓ I choose to see the world through a lens of positivity and optimism.

- ✓ I express gratitude for even the smallest blessings in my life.

- ✓ I cultivate a positive mindset and attract positive experiences into my life.

- ✓ I surround myself with positivity and uplifting energy.

- ✓ I am a magnet for abundance and blessings.

✓ I spread positivity and kindness wherever I go.

✓ I am grateful for the challenges that have helped me grow and learn.

✓ I trust that everything happens for a reason and that good things are coming my way.

Chapter 9: Affirmations for Mindfulness and Presence

ॐ (Om)

- ✓ I am fully present in this moment, and savor the beauty around me.

- ✓ I breathe deeply and release any tension or stress in my body.

- ✓ I let go of worries about the future and regrets about the past, and focus on the present.

- ✓ I engage my senses fully, and appreciate the sights, sounds, and sensations of the world around me.

- ✓ I practice mindfulness in all my activities and interactions.

- ✓ I take time to pause and reflect on my thoughts and emotions.

- ✓ I am aware of the impact of my thoughts and emotions on my well-being.

- ✓ I am centered and grounded in my being, and trust my inner wisdom.

✓ I am grateful for the gift of mindfulness and presence, and cultivate it daily.

✓ I embrace the present moment as the only moment that truly exists.

Chapter 10: Affirmations for Spirituality and Connection

ॐ (Om)

✓ I am connected to a higher power that guides me on my journey.

✓ I am grateful for the blessings and miracles that come from the universe.

- ✓ I trust that I am on the path that is meant for me, and that all will unfold as it should.

- ✓ I find peace and comfort in my spiritual practices and beliefs.

- ✓ I cultivate a sense of oneness with all living beings and the world around me.

- ✓ I practice compassion and kindness towards all, knowing that we are all interconnected.

- ✓ I seek to understand the mysteries of the universe and the purpose of my existence.

- ✓ I am open to new spiritual experiences and practices that resonate with my soul.

- ✓ I honor and respect all religious and spiritual beliefs, knowing that they are paths to the same truth.

- ✓ I am grateful for the sense of connection and purpose that spirituality brings to my life.

Chapter 11: Affirmations for Creativity and Expression

ॐ (Om)

- ✓ I am a creative being, and my imagination knows no limits.

- ✓ I trust in my ability to create and express myself in unique and authentic ways.

- ✓ I honor and respect my creative voice and allow it to flow freely.

- ✓ I find joy and fulfillment in the process of creating, and not just the outcome.

- ✓ I embrace mistakes and imperfections as part of the creative process, and learn from them.

- ✓ I am open to new ideas and inspiration that expand my creative horizons.

- ✓ I celebrate the diversity of creative expression in the world, and find inspiration in it.

- ✓ I express myself confidently and fearlessly, knowing that my voice matters.

- ✓ I am grateful for the gift of creativity, and use it to uplift and inspire others.

- ✓ I trust that my creative expression has the power to change the world.

Chapter 12: Affirmations for Growth and Learning

ॐ (Om)

- ✓ I am committed to lifelong learning and growth, knowing that it is essential to my well-being.

- ✓ I embrace new challenges and experiences that stretch me beyond my comfort zone.

- ✓ I cultivate a growth mindset and believe that my abilities can always be developed and improved.

- ✓ I seek out opportunities to learn from others, and value diverse perspectives

- ✓ I am open to feedback and constructive criticism, knowing that it helps me grow and improve.

- ✓ I approach mistakes as opportunities for growth and learning, rather than as failures.

- ✓ I trust in my ability to overcome obstacles and challenges, and to come out stronger on the other side.

- ✓ I embrace uncertainty and change as natural parts of life, and use them as opportunities for growth.

- ✓ I am committed to personal development and self-improvement, and take intentional steps towards it.
- ✓ I am grateful for the opportunities for growth and learning that come my way.

Chapter 13: Affirmations for Courage and Resilience

ॐ (Om)

- ✓ I am courageous and resilient, and face challenges with strength and determination.

- ✓ I trust in my inner strength and resourcefulness to overcome any obstacle.

✓ I am not defined by my past mistakes or failures, but by my ability to rise above them.

✓ I believe in myself and my abilities, and take bold action towards my goals and dreams.

✓ I embrace fear as a natural part of the human experience, and use it as a motivator to take action.

✓ I surround myself with people who uplift and support me in my journey.

✓ I am resilient in the face of adversity, and use it as an opportunity for growth.

✓ I trust that everything will work out for my highest good, even in the face of uncertainty and challenge.

✓ I am grateful for the strength and courage that I possess, and use it to inspire others.

✓ I believe that I can overcome any challenge and achieve anything I set my mind to.

<u>**Chapter 14: Affirmations for Love and Relationships**</u>

ॐ (Om)

- ✓ I am worthy of love and belonging, and attract positive and fulfilling relationships into my life.

- ✓ I approach relationships with honesty, openness, and vulnerability.

- ✓ I practice empathy and compassion towards others, knowing that we all have our struggles.

- ✓ I communicate my needs and boundaries clearly and respectfully, and honor those of others.

✓ I am grateful for the love and support of my friends and family.

✓ I am open to new relationships and connections, and trust in the power of human connection.

✓ I respect and honor the diversity of relationships and love in the world, and find inspiration in it.

✓ I approach love and relationships with an open heart, and without fear or judgment.

✓ I am committed to creating positive and fulfilling relationships in my life.

✓ I believe in the power of love to transform and heal the world.

Chapter 15: Affirmations for Gratitude and Abundance

ॐ (Om)

- ✓ I am grateful for the abundance of blessings in my life, both big and small.

- ✓ I approach life with a mindset of abundance and trust in the universe to provide for me.

- ✓ I appreciate the simple pleasures of life and find joy in them.

- ✓ I express gratitude openly and often, and acknowledge the impact of others in my life.

- ✓ I am grateful for the challenges and struggles that have helped me grow and learn.

- ✓ I recognize that abundance is not just material possessions, but also includes love, health, and happiness.

✓ I practice generosity and give freely of my time, resources, and talents.

✓ I believe that there is enough abundance in the world for everyone, and that we can all thrive.

✓ I attract abundance into my life by staying positive, focused, and taking intentional action towards my goals.
✓ I am grateful for the abundance and blessings that continue to flow into my life.

Chapter 16: Affirmations for Joy and Playfulness

ॐ (Om)

✓ I embrace joy and playfulness as essential parts of a fulfilling life.

- ✓ I approach life with a childlike sense of wonder and

- ✓ I allow myself to be silly and have fun, even in serious situations.

- ✓ I find joy in simple pleasures and activities, like spending time in nature or laughing with friends.

- ✓ I prioritize activities that bring me joy and allow me to fully express myself.

- ✓ I approach challenges with a positive and lighthearted attitude, knowing that laughter can be the best medicine.

- ✓ I surround myself with people who bring joy and positivity into my life.

- ✓ I believe that laughter and joy are contagious, and strive to spread them to others.

- ✓ I am grateful for the joy and happiness that I experience in my life.

✓ I approach life with a sense of playfulness and curiosity, always seeking new experiences and adventures.

Chapter 17: Affirmations for Self-Care and Self-Love

ॐ (Om)

✓ I prioritize my physical, emotional, and mental health through self-care practices.

✓ I am kind and compassionate towards myself, knowing that I am doing the best I can.

✓ I recognize and honor my boundaries and needs, and communicate them clearly to others.

✓ I make time for activities and practices that nourish my soul and bring me joy.

✓ I approach self-care as a lifelong journey, and am committed to making it a priority in my life.

✓ I practice self-love and acceptance, embracing all aspects of myself, including my flaws and imperfections.

✓ I believe in my own worth and value, and refuse to settle for anything less than I deserve.

✓ I am patient and understanding with myself, knowing that growth and healing take time.

✓ I am grateful for the opportunity to practice self-care and self-love, and to show up as my best self in the world.

✓ I am committed to prioritizing my own needs and well-being, knowing that it is essential for a fulfilling life.

Chapter 18: Affirmations for Spirituality and Connection

ॐ (Om)

- ✓ I believe in the power of connection, both with myself and with others.

- ✓ I recognize and honor the divine within myself and others, knowing that we are all connected.

- ✓ I approach spirituality as a personal journey, and am open to exploring different beliefs and practices.

- ✓ I practice gratitude and mindfulness, recognizing the beauty and sacredness in everyday moments.

- ✓ I honor my intuition and inner guidance, trusting that it will lead me towards my highest good.

✓ I approach challenges and obstacles with a sense of faith and trust in the universe.

✓ I find inspiration and guidance in the natural world, and feel connected to its rhythms and cycles.

✓ I believe in the power of prayer and meditation to connect with the divine and find inner peace.

✓ I am grateful for the spiritual connections and experiences in my life, and strive to deepen them.

✓ I believe that spirituality is an essential part of a fulfilling life, and am committed to nurturing my own connection with the divine.

Chapter 19: Affirmations for Purpose and Meaning

ॐ (Om)

- ✓ I believe that I have a unique purpose and mission in the world.

- ✓ I approach life with a sense of curiosity and wonder, always seeking to discover my true purpose.

- ✓ I am open to new experiences and opportunities that may lead me towards my purpose.

- ✓ I trust in the universe to guide me towards my highest good and fulfill my purpose.

- ✓ I find meaning and purpose in serving others and making a positive impact in the world.

- ✓ I approach challenges and obstacles as opportunities to grow and learn, and to fulfill my purpose.

- ✓ I am grateful for the opportunities to fulfill my purpose and make a positive impact in the world.

✓ I believe that everyone has a unique purpose and mission in the world, and strive to support others

Chapter 20: Affirmations for Wealth and Abundance

ॐ (Om)

✓ I am worthy of abundance and prosperity in all areas of my life, including my finances.

✓ I approach money with a positive and abundance mindset, knowing that there is always enough to go around.

✓ I believe that abundance is my birthright, and am open to receiving all the wealth and abundance the universe has in store for me.

✓ I am grateful for the money and resources that I have, and use them wisely and responsibly.

✓ I attract wealth and abundance into my life effortlessly and easily.

✓ I release any limiting beliefs or fears around money, and embrace a mindset of abundance and prosperity.

✓ I am open to receiving unexpected sources of income and opportunities for financial growth.

✓ I believe that I am capable of achieving financial freedom and abundance, and take actions towards that goal every day.

✓ I surround myself with people who support my financial goals and inspire me to grow.

✓ I am grateful for the abundance and prosperity in my life, and use it to make a positive impact in the world.

Chapter 21: Affirmations for Financial Growth and Success

ॐ (Om)

✓ I am capable of achieving my financial goals and dreams, and take consistent action towards them.

✓ I believe in my ability to create wealth and financial abundance in my life.

✓ I approach financial growth with a mindset of curiosity and learning, always seeking to improve my knowledge and skills.

✓ I am open to taking risks and trying new approaches to achieve financial success.

- ✓ I release any limiting beliefs or fears around success and financial growth, and embrace a mindset of possibility and abundance.

- ✓ I believe that my financial success will benefit not only myself but also those around me.

- ✓ I am grateful for the opportunities to grow and succeed financially, and am committed to using my wealth and resources to make a positive impact in the world.

- ✓ I attract financial opportunities and success into my life effortlessly and easily.

- ✓ I am open to receiving guidance and support from others who have achieved financial success.

- ✓ I approach financial growth with a long-term perspective, knowing that it requires patience, persistence, and consistent action.

Chapter 22: Affirmations for Financial Responsibility and Abundance

ॐ (Om)

- ✓ I am responsible and mindful with my money and finances, using them in a way that aligns with my values and goals.

- ✓ I approach money as a tool for creating abundance and making a positive impact in the world.

- ✓ I am open to giving and receiving in equal measure, knowing that abundance is a flow of energy.

- ✓ I prioritize saving and investing in my future financial growth and stability.

- ✓ I release any guilt or shame around money, knowing that it is a neutral tool that can be used for good or bad.

✓ I am grateful for the financial abundance in my life, and use it to create a life of joy, purpose, and fulfillment.

✓ I am committed to using my financial resources to support causes and organizations that align with my values and make a positive impact in the world.

✓ I approach financial responsibility with a sense of empowerment and confidence, knowing that I am in control of my financial destiny.

✓ I attract abundance and financial opportunities into my life effortlessly and easily.

✓ I believe that financial abundance and responsibility are not mutually exclusive, and strive to cultivate both in my life.

Congratulations on completing this book on healthy affirmations! By now, you should have a good understanding of how affirmations work and how to use them to improve your health and well-being. Remember that affirmations are a powerful tool, but they work best when used in combination with other healthy habits, such as eating well, exercising, and getting enough sleep.

It's also important to be patient and kind to yourself as you embark on this journey. Change doesn't happen overnight, and it's normal to experience setbacks and challenges along the way. But by staying committed to your goals and using affirmations to reinforce your positive mindset, you'll get closer and closer to the healthy, happy life you desire.

Thank you for reading.

Thankyou Note

I wanted to especially thank my parents, friends, and teachers for their support in helping me create this book. Their words of encouragement, love, and positivity have been instrumental in shaping my mindset and outlook towards life. With their help, I was able to compile a collection of affirmations that resonate with me on a personal level and have helped me overcome challenges and obstacles.

Every time I read through the pages of this book, I am reminded of the power of positivity and the importance of having a supportive network of people around me. I feel blessed to have such amazing individuals in my life who believe in me and inspire me to be the best version of myself.

Once again, I cannot thank you enough for this thoughtful gift and for the role that each of you has played in making it possible. Your kindness and generosity mean the world to me.

With heartfelt thanks

100RAB

www.ingramcontent.com/pod-product-compliance
Lightning Source LLC
Chambersburg PA
CBHW031247130726
47988CB00008B/3282